BUZZ

A book of happiness for bee lovers

Compiled by Adam Langstroth

EXISLE
PUBLISHING

Introduction

Bees are fun to watch and a delight to listen to. They're endlessly fascinating and very photogenic.

The lives of bees and humans are intricately intertwined. The bee symbol was part of the Egyptian hieroglyphic language; Hindu gods are often associated with bees; the Quran records specific instructions to bees; there are references to bees in the Bible; and Buddhists point out that the bee does no harm, instead taking only what is needed. Greeks, Romans and other ancient civilizations all admired the industry, organization and hierarchical structure of bee life. Napoleon adopted the bee as his symbol. And today the bee is a style inspiration for fabrics, jewellery and even architecture.

Throughout our history, most people have generally taken bees for granted. But now they are under pressure. Writers and conservationists have worked hard to raise our awareness of their plight, and nowadays no respectable community is far from a few hives. So progress is being made, but there is much more to do before our pollution, pesticides, water sprinklers, monocropping, and general 'tidying up' — to name just a few threats — eliminate them. If bees are not helped by humans their extinction will be that much closer. We can all take simple steps to help them. If you can't have hives, then grow bee-friendly plants. Avoid sprinklers and pesticides, and have spaces where they can safely gather water.

Despite their critical importance for human survival, there are remarkably few quotes about bees. The same ones tend to appear time and again in quote books, blogs and other sources. It seems humans talk more often about celebrities and political leaders and forget who actually does the work! So you won't find bees listed in the index of most major biographies, and there are no superstar beekeepers, but it would be wise to remember that their profession is nobler than most.

Handle a book as a bee does
a flower, extract its sweetness
but do not damage it.

JOHN MUIR

Bees have so much to offer us
if we only listen.

JAY EBBEN

To an intelligent and candid mind the smallest piece of honey-comb is a perfect demonstration that there is a 'GREAT FIRST CAUSE'.

LANGSTROTH

Beauty will save the world.

FYODOR DOSTOEVSKY

Your home should tell the story of who you are, and be a collection of what you love brought together under one roof.

NATE BERKUS

O bees, sing soft, and,
bees, sing low;
For she is gone who
loved you so.

EUGENE FIELD

Be it ever so humble there's
no place like home.

PROVERB

And the bumble bees kept bumbling
away among the flowers ...

C.G. LELAND

There's honey in the leaf
and the blossom,
And honey in the night and the day.

KATHARINE TYNAN HINKSON

The only reason for being a bee that I know of is to make honey. And the only reason for making honey is so I can eat it.

WINNIE-THE-POOH

And great bees come,
with their sleepy tune,
To sip their honey and circle round.

P.B. MARSTON

Order is Heaven's first law.

ALEXANDER POPE

Bees that have honey in their mouths
have stings in their tails.

PROVERB

Give me a 15-foot crocodile
any day over a bee.

BINDI IRWIN

So the industrious bees
do hourly strive
To bring their loads of honey
to the hive.

MARY COLLIER

The honeybee, *Apis mellifera*, is a species on the cusp of culture and nature … If we're to seriously improve honeybee health and with it our own wellbeing, we need to make the most of this timely opportunity to realise a more interconnected approach to agriculture and ecology.

SARAH WARING, *FARMING FOR THE LANDLESS: NEW PERSPECTIVES ON THE CULTIVATION OF OUR HONEYBEE*

Collaboration is the essence of life.
The wind, bees and flowers work
together to spread the pollen.

AMIT RAY

Mist to mist, drops to drops.
For water thou art, and unto water
shalt thou return.

KAMAND KOJOURI

Who are you running from,
you crazy man? …
Even gods have lived in the
woods like me.

VIRGIL

If bees only gathered nectar from perfect flowers, they wouldn't be able to make even a single drop of honey.

MATSHONA DHLIWAYO

For so work the honey-bees,
Creatures that by a rule in nature teach
The act of order to a peopled kingdom.

WILLIAM SHAKESPEARE, *HENRY V*

The hum of bees is the voice
of the garden.

ELIZABETH LAWRENCE

One can no more approach
people without love than one
can approach bees without care.
Such is the quality of bees ...

LEO TOLSTOY

Bees do have a smell, you know,
and if they don't they should, for
their feet are dusted with spices
from a million flowers.

RAY BRADBURY

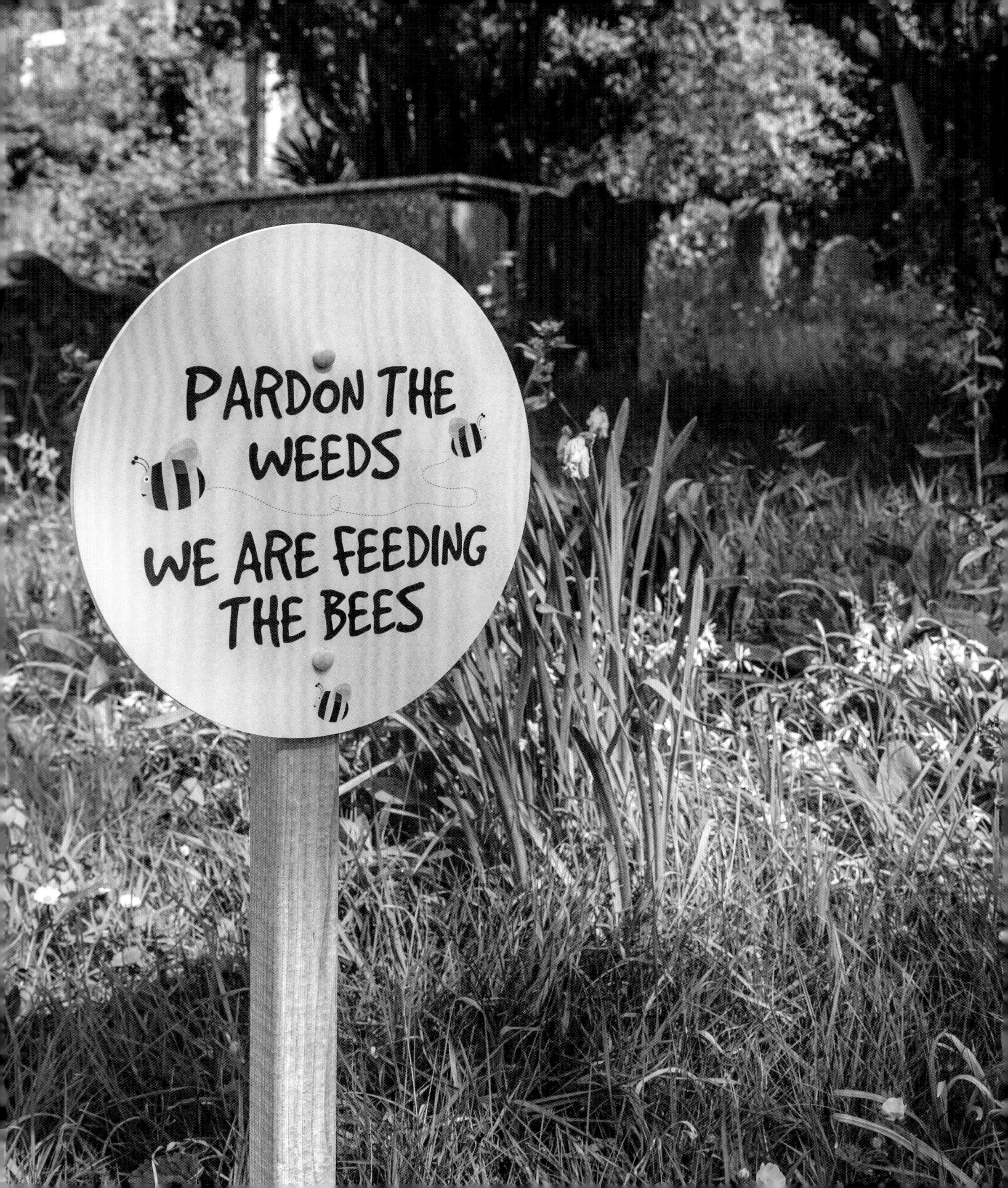
PARDON THE
WEEDS
WE ARE FEEDING
THE BEES

A clear purpose will unite you
as you move forward,
values will guide your behaviour,
and goals will focus your energy.

KENNETH H. BLANCHARD

The happiness of the bee and
the dolphin is to exist.
For man it is to know that and
to wonder at it.

JACQUES YVES COUSTEAU

The moan of doves
in immemorial elms
And murmuring of
innumerable bees.

ALFRED, LORD TENNYSON

Bees ... by virtue of a certain geometrical forethought ... know that the hexagon is greater than the square and the triangle, and will hold more honey for the same expenditure of material.

PAPPUS OF ALEXANDRIA

Four eyes see more than two. (But how about five?)

PROVERB (NOT)

The bee is domesticated
but not tamed.

WILLIAM LONGGOOD

When the flower blossoms,
the bee will come.

SRIKUMAR RAO

Go abroad and you'll hear
news of home.

PROVERB

Did you know that honey bees came
over with the Pilgrims?
They are not recognized as citizens
but corporations are!

JUNE STOYER

The busy bee has no time for sorrow.

WILLIAM BLAKE

The life of a swarm of bees is like an active and hazardous campaign of an army: the ranks are being continually depleted and continually recruited.

JOHN BURROUGHS

Nine bean-rows will I have there,
a hive for the honey-bee,
And live alone in the bee-loud glade

W.B. YEATS

The cells of the bees are found
perfectly to answer all the most
refined conditions of a very
intricate mathematical problem!

LANGSTROTH

O, beautiful damsel, tell me the
number of bees.

HENRY WADSWORTH LONGFELLOW

Instead of worrying about what you cannot control, shift your energy to what you can create.

ROY T. BENNETT

With the hum of swarming bees
Into dreamful slumber lull'd.

ALFRED, LORD TENNYSON

The bee sucks honey out of the
bitterest flowers.

PROVERB

No living creature, not even
man, has achieved in the centre
of his sphere, what the bee has
achieved in her own.

MAURICE MAETERLINCK

One swallow will not make spring,
nor one bee honey.

PROVERB

How skilfully she builds her cell!
How neat she spreads the wax!

ISAAC WATTS

The bees go booming
through the flats of flowers.

THE HON. MRS NORTON,
THE LADY OF LA GARAYE

If the bee disappeared off the
face of the earth, man would
only have four years left to live.

MAURICE MAETERLINCK

Bees are the batteries of orchards,
gardens, guard them.

CAROL ANN DUFFY

If you want to find the secrets of the universe, think in terms of energy, frequency and vibration.

NIKOLA TESLA

Beauty is not in the face; beauty is a light in the heart.

KAHLIL GIBRAN

There will never be a 'royal road' to profitable bee-keeping. If there is any branch of rural economy which more than all others demands care and experience, for its profitable management, it is the keeping of bees …

LANGSTROTH

You voluble,
Velvety
Vehement fellows.

NORMAN ROWLAND GALE

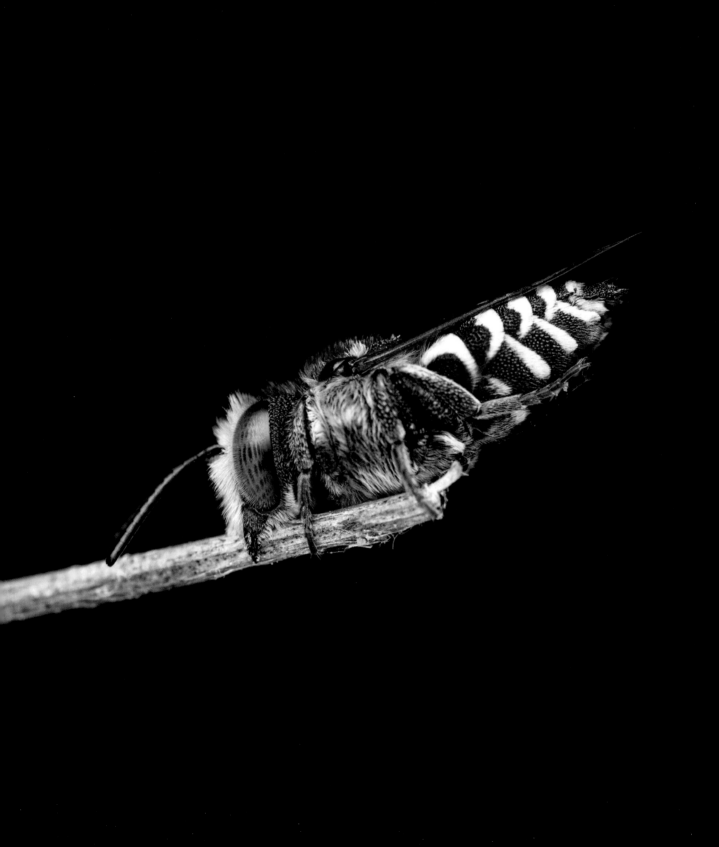

We ascribe beauty to that which is simple; which has no superfluous parts; which exactly answers its ends.

RALPH WALDO EMMERSON

You can have everything you want if you can put your heart and soul into everything you do.

ROY T. BENNETT

Work is much more fun than fun.

NOËL COWARD

Trust one who has gone through it.

VIRGIL

Lovely enchanting language,
sugar-cane,
Honey of roses, wither wilt thou fly?

GEORGE HERBERT

The most laborious of all insects,
if compared with the rest, are the
tribes of ants and bees.

ARISTOTLE

Where bees are, there is honey.

PROVERB

That which is not good for
the bee-hive cannot be good
for the bees.

MARCUS AURELIUS

Where the bee sucks honey
the spider sucks poison.

PROVERB

Take care of your costume
and your confidence will
take care of itself.

AMIT KALANTRI

Let there be spaces in your togetherness.

KAHLIL GIBRAN

The bee is more honoured
than other animals, not because
she labours, but because she
labours for others.

SAINT JOHN CHRYSOSTOM

How doth the little busy bee
Improve each shining hour,
And gather honey all the day
From every opening flower!

ISAAC WATTS

Consider well the proportion of things.

MARK TWAIN

Honey is sweet, but the bee stings.

PROVERB

The bee's life is like a magic well:
the more you draw from it, the
more it fills with water.

KARL VON FRISCH

What we play is life.

LOUIS ARMSTRONG

Honey is not for the ass's mouth.

PROVERB

I wait for form.

ROBERT FROST

Listen to the bees
and let them guide you.

BROTHER ADAM

Never did I behold thee so attired
And garmented in beauty as to-night!
What hast thou done to make thee
look so fair?

HENRY WADSWORTH LONGFELLOW,
THE SPANISH STUDENT

He is not worthy of the honey-comb, that shuns the hives because the bees have stings.

WILLIAM SHAKESPEARE

The lovely flowers embarrass.
They make me regret I am not a bee.

EMILY DICKINSON

The keeping of bees is like the
direction of sunbeams.

HENRY DAVID THOREAU

The only way round is through.

ROBERT FROST